Stoic Meditations

The Daily Stoic Ways to Think Like A Roman Emperor - Meditations on Wisdom, Perseverance, and the Art of Living

Marcus Epictetus

© Copyright 2021 Marcus Epictetus - All rights reserved.

The content contained within this book may not be reproduced, duplicated or transmitted without direct written permission from the author or the publisher.

Under no circumstances will any blame or legal responsibility be held against the publisher, or author, for any damages, reparation, or monetary loss due to the information contained within this book, either directly or indirectly.

Legal Notice:

This book is copyright protected. It is only for personal use. You cannot amend, distribute, sell, use, quote or paraphrase any part, or the content within this book, without the consent of the author or publisher.

Disclaimer Notice:

Please note the information contained within this document is for educational and entertainment purposes only. All effort has been executed to present accurate, up to date, reliable, complete information. No warranties of any kind are declared or implied. Readers acknowledge that the author is not engaging in the rendering of legal, financial, medical or professional advice. The content within this book has been derived from various sources. Please consult a licensed professional before attempting any techniques outlined in this book.

By reading this document, the reader agrees that under no circumstances is the author responsible for any losses, direct or indirect, that are incurred as a result of the use of information contained within this document, including, but not limited to, errors, omissions, or inaccuracies.

Content

Introduction 1

Chapter 1: Stoic Practices – Good or Bad? 9

Chapter 2: Emotions! 26

Chapter 3: Principles of Stoicism 41

Chapter 4: Psychological Resilience 60

Chapter 5: Modern Day Practices 74

Chapter 6: Meditation 88

Chapter 7: Becoming a Modern Stoic 101

Conclusion 116

Thank you! 123

Check Out My Other Books 124

Introduction

The book "Stoic guide for beginners" is written to help you comprehend the existence of ancient philosophy and how it can help you in your modern-day life. It focuses on the understanding that what we cannot control, such as our health or wealth, is outside our power or influence. This aspect can be hard to understand because things like losing a loved one and not being wealthy are unavoidable. Stoicism's idea is to use logic and reasoning to determine how we should react to these events with dignity instead of overwhelming sorrow and anger because they are out of our control. Stoics believe that people who feel emotions when faced with nameless obstacles are weak, but those who stay calm under any circumstance have the strength inside them.

Modern-day philosophers are still debating Stoicism's moral value and its potential for living a happy, fulfilling life. However, Stoicism's broad consensus as it was understood in ancient Athens does not work well with modern society, but it can if understood and reciprocated well enough. It is a philosophy that started in Ancient Greece and developed with its influence spreading over Western culture. Stoic philosophy's general belief is the ability to experience life through apatheia (Philosophy) or tranquil indifference towards disinteresting things not under one's control, combined with living according to virtue.

Ancient philosophy is different from the modern-day because ancient philosophers focused more on the spiritual aspect of life, whereas early thinkers focused more on the material. Ancient philosophers believed that there was a higher way of thinking than pure logic and common sense. These are some critical differences between ancient philosophy and modern-day philosophies.

Stoicism teaches people how to think about and deal with pain, suffering, and, misfortune. Zeno of Citium developed this study in Athens around 300 BC. The Stoics believed that the only good is virtue and everything else - money, power, health - merely serves as a means to obtain it. They also believed human beings are naturally sociable creatures who live together harmoniously in society when they do not allow themselves to be controlled by their passions or desires for material things.

If you are interested in stoicism, then this book can help guide you. Learn more about how to use Stoic teachings to improve your life and help take control of the direction of your destiny. Commonly called 'living worldly' or 'natural' (depending on the translation), Stoicism emphasizes a rational philosophy based on what we know today as cognitive behavioral therapy. In other words, negative emotions come from erroneous belief systems, and real knowledge obtained through human reasoning helps us build insight into our emotional lives

Modern proponents claim that Stoicism offers a practical guide to eudaimonia in the form of psychological and ethical precepts for guiding one's actions (Mastery, "Stoic Philosophy"). Unlike most schools of thought, it applies equally well as therapy for anxiety disorders or helps recover from a traumatic experience given its promotion of psychologically informed practices such as meditation.

We investigate what stoicism means in a modern-day context, the systems developed by ancient stoics to help them overcome their perceived obstacles to happiness, and strategies for applying these principles during Jiddu Krishnamurti's life

Traces of this discipline can be found throughout secular literature. It has also influenced many religious movements such as Buddhism Essays have been written on the concept, practices, and history. It is discussed in Pascal's Pensées (1670), Kant's Critique of Practical Reason (1788). The law is rooted in Western culture and finds.

Most of what we hear about philosophy is abstract musings and impractical thinking, but Stoicism was primarily concerned with understanding human nature and applying it in practical ways. It was founded by Zeno of Citium in the 3rd century BC.

Stoicism is a Hellenistic school that flourished throughout the Roman and Greek world until the 3rd century AD. Among its most notable adherents were emperor Marcus Aurelius, philosophers Epictetus and Musonius Rufus, satirist Lucian of Samosata, and slave-turned-rhetorician Maximus of Tyre. Stoic doctrines varied over time, but they tended to stress humanism, respect for others (excluding slaves), honorable intentions ("non malificam"), and the pursuit of virtue as a means to attain a happy life

In the last few years, stoicism has gained momentum across the world. In 2009, there were ten books on Stoic philosophy, and in 2011 it increased to 40. Additionally, there are many clubs, groups, and meetups with regular attendees who gather to practice these moral beliefs.

However, even though more and more people claim that they follow a range of core values: poverty was believed an evil by 64% of people at the time (compared to 78% who accepted the idea as accurate in 1999), personal honesty became 84%, charity 83%, and physical courage 76%.

On the positive side, training in Stoicism can help us develop an awareness of our impact on others. This is a leadership skill much needed today. We all have numerous encounters with other people each day. Our words and actions affect them powerfully even when we are not aware we are doing so. Training in Stoic philosophy can help the US to be more conscientious of that effect, both for good or ill

Almost any problem in life can be avoided by not being there, to begin with. Do this, and you will remain invulnerable – save for perhaps a few inevitable misfortunes, which cannot be helped if one is trying very hard to stay somewhere else. Therefore, the Stoic makes sure that he has all the resources within him necessary to deal with whatever seems likely enough on his horizon to need bearing in mind. Likewise, too much thinking time spent dwelling upon possible misfortunes is simply wasted energy.

How to Use This Book

Stoic Guide for beginners is a short book designed to give you some simple strategies for overcoming problems and dealing with emotions. It's written to help people deal with their anxiety disorders and depression, resulting from a crippling inability to deal with daily problems, social aggression, lack of attention span, and forgetfulness.

No matter what the problem is, the root of emotional instability is the same. Whether you wonder why you cannot get a job or feel like no one understands you, this book will guide you in figuring out the issue for yourself. As long as we know our flaws and strengths and we are willing to work on them - then there is no telling where we will be in the end!

Many authors want to teach new readers about this ancient philosophy, but it cannot be apparent for beginners who do not know where to start. This book will help the reader go from novice to expert and begin practicing stoic exercises immediately!

The author has created an easy-to-follow guide teaching everything you need to know to get started practicing stoic exercises right away. You will learn why stoicism is useful today, some of its histories, and most importantly

- what exactly are these exercises that have been proven effective over 2000 years? This book delves into specific techniques that will alter your mental state, allowing you to think better, focus more on things that matter, and eliminate distractions.

So, let us begin our journey into learning more about stoicism

Chapter 1: Stoic Practices – Good or Bad?

There are many schools of thought. Some schools have become more popular than others, and some are still in their nascent stages. However, all schools do not use good practice or bad practice to guide them. What is this concept? Moreover, how can you use it to your advantage?

There are also schools of thought for philosophy as well as business. Some people say that you should focus on the customer first and foremost, while others might think that your employees should be given priority. The two schools of thought that will result in success for any company are balancing both sides: treat your customers well and take care of your staff to perform at their optimum level.

In the case of Schools for thought in Philosophy, the first was Plato's Academy, a school that he founded and ran for over 30 years. This school was dedicated to the pursuit of knowledge and truth through philosophical discussion. Its most famous student was Aristotle, who would later find his academy and author some of the most influential books in philosophy today, like "The Nicomachean Ethics." Another vital school is Stoicism, which argues that humans should learn how to overcome fear and pain by accepting them with dignity instead of trying to escape from them or fight against them. There is also Existentialism whose goal is not necessarily absolute truth but instead searching for meaning within oneself despite any objective reality outside one's self. However, there can be no ultimate moral authority on what life means to human beings since they all have different perspectives based on their experiences.

However, how can you tell the difference between a good practice and a bad one? A good Stoic knows how to make the most out of any situation they have a good grasp of their emotions, no matter what circumstance they are in. A good stoic can learn to be content with what he has since he believes that his wants and needs will come when appropriate.

Often people run around aimlessly around trying to find happiness and fulfillment but never really succeeding. In doing this, people have often forgotten about the core values of Stoicism, a form of Philosophy from over 2 thousand years ago. A philosophy that teaches us how to live well despite lacking "things,".

This philosophy takes its name from the Stoa Poikilê, a porch for people to walk upon as they conversed in ancient Platonic Athens. This was where Zeno of Citium (c.334-262 BCE) taught Stoic philosophy among his fellow citizens who were returning home after their work-day, seeking refreshment with friends and practical exercises to help them transform themselves into better persons. Though Stoicism was briefly eclipsed by Epicureanism during Roman times, it returned when Epictetus began teaching at Rome around 100 CE.

Zeno developed most of the core.

Common Mistakes you can make.

Having misconceptions about stoicism is quite natural, and it does happen often. One familiar misconception people believe when thinking of Stoics is that they are emotionless, but it is very different. Stoics believe in experiencing emotions and feelings but not responding to them. Another misconception is that stoics do not talk or interact with other people when they can be exceptionally social! There is more to being stoic than just sitting there looking like you are thinking all the time deeply.

This ancient philosophy focuses on wisdom and being in harmony with the world. Despite lacking dogmatic premises, it can teach you important life lessons if practiced correctly. This book will tell you about critical points of stoic theory like "The four pillars" and how to view the good life.

Understanding the virtues and respecting them make it easier to avoid common mistakes made by a person practicing Stoicism for the first time. However, even a person with experience can often fall victim to their emotions, which is entirely okay. Getting out of a negative situation is one of the essential aspects of Stoicism.

It is a practical philosophy that's much easier to use than it sounds. There are seemingly countless ways the theory can be applied, and yet many people still get confused and discouraged by this philosophy because they make mistakes in practice. "Stoic guide for beginners" intends to clear up common misunderstandings and remove the roadblocks that prevent modern people from using this powerful and ancient wisdom.

When practicing this philosophy, people can make errors and not effectively use them to achieve a better day. The most common mistakes in these circumstances are: suppressing emotions, sacrificing pleasure, and using this philosophy as an excuse to hurt others emotionally.

It is common for people to misconstrue Stoicism's concept, and often they will not follow through with what it entails. The first mistake made by people practicing Stoicism in the modern-day and age is that they don't take their emotions into account when deliberating on a situation. One principle of Stoic philosophy is that one should maintain ataraxia, which means "peacefulness" or "tranquility." This aspect comes from an understanding of virtue as a form of inner strength. It is about facing difficult circumstances without feeling fear or anger but instead resigning oneself to facing the difficulties head-on with courage and dignity. Epictetus, a Greek philosopher who practiced Stoicism, said: "What are your desires? To have things done according to your will? Well, then do so! Take control of yourself!"

Being a better person is key; hurting someone else for your benefit is not accepted in this philosophical teaching.

Develop Internal Locus of Control

Do you feel that external forces control your life? Do you seem to have little or no control over the events of your life? Imagine what it would be like if, at any moment, you could direct the outcome toward something useful.

Internal or externally control-oriented people should read more on the concept, "locus of control." The concepts underlying locus-of-control are empirical and straightforward to study; they can be applied in the clinical situation and the classroom, and within families. Recently some revised versions have appeared that test for differences between achievement and power orientations.

This idea seems far-fetched for many people, but Stoicism has taught people how to do just that for centuries. This philosophy has taught wisdom from thousands of years ago to help develop an internal locus of control.

This practice talks extensively about the degree to which a person believes they have control over their own life. Julian Rotter coined the term in 1954. He created six different loci of control: Personal, Chance, Powerful Others, Society or Social Institutions, Uncontrollable or Ill-Fated Events (sometimes called Learned Helplessness), and Mystical Forces.

It is a term that expresses the degree to which people believe they have control over their own life. He often explained why some cultures seem more prone to externalizing others' problems, such as blaming the government or other people, rather than taking responsibility themselves. It is also thought to be one factor responsible for specific personality disorders like paranoia and narcissism.

It is often referred to as "internal" or "external." An external locus of control means you think outside forces make your decisions, whereas an internal locus of control means you believe it's up to you. Practicing an internal locus can help you focus on goals and feel more secure about yourself.

Negative Visualization

Practicing Stoic disciplines such as negative visualization (imagining your worst fears coming true) or voluntary discomfort (doing something uncomfortable) trains us not to be frightened by events that are actually unlikely or even impossible.

The Stoic philosophy of living in harmony with nature, while not always having absolute control over our external circumstances, was the first systematic human psychology and provided a unique framework for seeing life's difficulties. Fewer people use it correctly these days, and even fewer use it as more than just a coping mechanism or 'philosophy-of-life. 'Stoicism is beneficial for maintaining emotional stability – which is enough for most people who fear they are on an extremist path.

According to researchers of happiness and human thriving, the key lies in Stoic philosophy! Specifically, because it involves wisdom from Marcus Aurelius, Zeno of Citium, Epictetus and Seneca focusing on teachings that make people more focused.

They discovered that we should control our desires, not let them control us – with good reason too. One must look past simple pleasure by avoiding anything external but your character and personality. We all have natural emotions, so if you manage these effectively, then a happier life follows. With additional benefits of fewer negative thoughts influencing decisions, which are great things to avoid when making choices.

Philosopher Massimo Pigliucci once discussed Stoicism along with the author Lawrence Becker. During the conversation between the two philosophers and academics, they explore such questions as "What is a practicing Stoic's relationship to fear?" Much of their discussion focuses on negative Visualization as well. This practice encourages us to spend some time imagining bad situations regularly. The concept of this technique is to imagine a life outside one's current lifestyle with everything going wrong and then realizing how much better one's own life is. This could be achieved through imagining what would happen if financial stability were lost or a loved one passed away. It has been argued that people who use this are left feeling okay about their current lives because they have imagined worse scenarios and survived them.

This powerful technique helped Stoic Philosophers achieve peace of mind. This exercise can also help people identify shortcomings so that we know where we need to improve. It has been shown that practicing this type of thinking can make people happier because it alleviates them from worrying about things going wrong. This procedure also helps people better appreciate the things that are currently working well in their lives.

Stoic Meditations

To practice this as you go about your day, spend some time now and then thinking in detail about the fact that you might lose all of your material possessions. Visualize what life would be like if everything was taken away from you today, tomorrow, or next week. You could also reflect on scenarios where a loved one could potentially die because that is just as likely to happen at any moment.

Where does it come from: This technique is based on advice Epictetus gave in Discourses 3-4 and which he later reiterated in Letter 10.

In short, this exercise intends to help you be more accepting of adverse outcomes and accept them graciously.

Marcus Aurelius, the Stoic Emperor of Rome, said to himself every morning, "You have power over your mind - not outside events. Realize this, and you will find strength". This inspirational affirmation encapsulates what it is to be a stoic; we control how we respond to situations, even if they are out of our control. There remains an element of choice in how we react concerning them. The Stoic Guide for Beginners: A Practical Guidebook for applying the ancient philosophy is - as its title suggests – a practical guide on understanding and practicing Stoicism.

Ideologies & Philosophers

The Stoics practiced their beliefs in judgment. They believed that a person of "moral and intellectual perfection" would not suffer the disturbance of emotions. This psychological training was an essential part of Stoic practice; as Musonius Rufus put it: "The goal of philosophy is life in agreement or harmony with nature. . .. We shall reach this aim if we think correctly about things divine and human.

Philosophy does not have to be staid, tedious, or difficult. Philosophy is a way of life that can positively transform your thoughts and actions. You can achieve this transformation by focusing on the words of notable philosophers, including Seneca (4 BCE-65 CE), Marcus Aurelius (121-180 ad), and Epictetus (50-120 ad). The Philosopher Statue from Dynamic Forces captures the visage of these thinkers perfectly.

Ideologies of Stoicism is a unique and self-created set of beliefs that drive an individual's behavior. The central tenets are imperviousness to strong emotions, indifference to death, taciturnity, and self-sufficiency. Stoicism's ideology may create an internal resistance to objective needs (Ladouceur et al., 2008). When applied in psychosocial aspects of healthcare settings such as communication with health professionals or coping with terminally ill situations, it can yield positive results.

The philosophy of Stoicism is thousands of years old. It aims to help you embrace a calm, happy life and achieve your potential by teaching you how to use reason to control the dangers that befall humans around them.

The Greeks broke down their philosophy into three parts: Logic, physics, and ethics. These Stoics philosophers lived around 300 BC in Greece and believed that to live well, one should accept that all human beings are subject to inevitable fate or destiny. Unlike Plato's idea of the reason being more critical than emotion (known as Platonism), the Stoics believed humans could live rationally by controlling their emotions through training over time.

These virtues are sometimes referred to as the four cardinal virtues: practical wisdom, moderation, courage, and justice. However, each of them individually is not considered a virtue in itself. However, they may be thought of as traits or dispositions that strengthen and ennoble humankind.

The Stoics sought after ethical notions and built principles. These eight principles of Stoicism are the foundation for living a good life. These principles have been used by people from all walks of life and can help you achieve your goals.

Stoic philosophy is about how to live well, not just exist. It is about being happy with what you have and using it wisely, rather than wanting more or wishing things were different. You will learn how to reason instead of emotionally to make better decisions in your daily life. This ideology will lead to greater happiness and fulfillment as well as improved relationships with others around you.

Stoic Meditations

Marcus Aurelius was a philosopher who lived in an age of chaos and war. From 154 to 161, he fought the Germanic tribes that were invading Rome. This Stoic Philosopher (121–180 CE): Marcus Aurelius was a Roman emperor. He ruled as part of the Antonine dynasty. He was the last of five emperors known collectively as the Five Good Emperors, whom each reigned for an average tenure of over two decades during a period in which the Empire reached its greatest extent under their rule.

He wrote "meditations"; Marcus Aurelius' book is considered one of the greatest works of philosophy ever written.

This famous source of information on Stoicism is a source for self-improvement. This book is about Marcus Aurelius's writings, recording his private notes and ideas on Stoic philosophy. This historical work has become one of the most read philosophical texts ever written with an enduring influence on Western pop culture.

He was also extensively known for his Stoic philosophy. Additionally, he became a noted polymath, leading the

Musaeum (a kind of research institute), writing poetry, and even doing meteorological observations and building an extensive canal system. However, Marcus Adulescens was best known as a conqueror; he extended Roman imperial rule further than any emperor before him – ultimately ruling over the entire Mediterranean region.

This colorless life-affirming biography ends on 21 May 180 when Marcus is in full command of his troops at Aquileia and

Another notable Stoic Philosopher was Zeno of Elea. The Stoic school of philosophy, which he taught in Athens from about 300 BC. Based on the moral ideas of the Cynics, Stoicism laid great emphasis on goodness and peace of mind gained from living a life of virtue following nature.

He was born −334 BCE (though there is debate over whether 336 or 324) in Citium, Cyprus. Virtually nothing is known about his early life, as he tells us nothing about himself. His name suggests a connection to Phoenicia.

His Dichotomy paradoxes are a specific set of paradoxical arguments that purport to show that motion is impossible or that change is illusory. Variants include the Arrow (or Achilles), which demonstrates the impossibility of motion; and several others. Over time many versions arose, with difficult-to-answer counterarguments by their advocates.

The contradictory reasoning behind this apparent paradox has been known since Antiquity but was fully formalized as part of classical logic in modern times, including consequent refutations.

Chapter 2: Emotions!

Are you feeling upset, guilty, or sad? You're not going crazy, and you honestly are fine. Physiologically speaking, these emotions serve a purpose: they let us know when we've done something wrong. If someone had this natural defense mechanism taken away- they wouldn't be able to learn from their mistakes without knowing something was wrong in the first place.

Can you quiet your mind amid the pressure of work? These are only some of the questions you ought to ask yourself instead.

Passion, anxiety, and fear are the symptoms of a life not lived according to nature. They are abnormal impulses, whereas feelings deriving from accurate perceptions of things by right reasoning belong to man's best interests and noblest capacities. For this reason, we should strive to banish passion, anxiety, and fear from our lives. So, if every time you lie, that feeling of dread just would go away – can you really say that life is better because it makes you feel less threatening?

Philosophers and psychologists have debated about emotions for centuries. One school state that emotions are a product of thoughts, while the other side argues they are an innate human characteristic. Some say that emotion has evolved to help us survive, while others argue it is merely a by-product of our brain's rational processes. While there may never be any concrete answer to it, we know one thing for sure, that they are still interesting to discuss!

The Stoic philosophers believe that emotions are not good or bad in themselves, but they come from a misunderstanding of the situation. This aspect is essential to understand because then we can choose our response to the situation and react. For example, if you are hungry and someone offers you food, they may have misinterpreted your hunger for being thirsty, so offer water instead of food. If you were thirsty, then this would be an appropriate reaction to your feelings. The Stoic philosophy also teaches us about how we should respond when things go wrong or turn out badly for us - what's done is done, and regret won't change anything, so there is no point dwelling on it!

People experience emotions as either negative or positive depending on their circumstances; however, Stoics do not think emotions are inherently good or bad but somewhat dependent upon our interpretation of them.

Let us think of a common emotion we all share, anger. Beautiful and desirable, yet dangerous at the same time, it's how often it happens to you in your daily life that makes this emotion different. A person who is continuously motivated to make choices depending on anger and emotions is not Stoic. Remember, the answer to mental instability in life is not reducing emotions; instead, redirecting them.

Philosophers have been examining anger since ancient times. Aristotle famously wrote about how the powerful should not show anger, but they are justified in using it for punishment if necessary. The Stoics argued that anger is an "irrational and unthinking passion." They believed that people needed to learn to control their emotions as much as possible to live a happy life.

People can also develop irrational fears related to specific situations, individuals, objects, or types of environment.

This phobia is called a social anxiety disorder, and people who experience this type of fear avoid interaction with other people for the duration of their life.

Stoicism can be used to deal with the ups and downs of everyday life. However, it is not suited for everyone. A stoic will feel good about undesirable events that happen in his or her life because he or she will, at that time, think of emotional growth. Joy is perhaps the most challenging emotion for someone who does not practice stoicism to understand.

Rather than avoiding emotion altogether, Stoic philosophy encourages us to deal wisely and constructively with all feelings – turning a potentially harmful stimulus into a positive challenge for growth."

The Discipline of Action

In ancient times, the Stoics studied wishing: how to wish well. According to their logic, it seems natural that one desires or wishes for oneself what is right. By extension, we will desire and wish well for everyone in turn (Aristotle would have said terrible people also likely shared this inclination). The most practical step was to get others to want something you know they would want if they were only told its benefits because this serves as a stepping stone towards eventually wanting it yourself.

One of Stoicism's fundamental tenets is that humans should have self-control and discipline themselves to be able to control their emotions and desires so they can focus on what matters most. The Discipline of Action in Stoicism allows for one's actions concerning external events not controlled by him, or she may be used as a guide for life.

This philosophy is not complicated or intensely personal practice. Stoicism intends to help you regulate emotions like anger, fear, anxiety, and jealousy without willpower in the ancient stoic manner. Instead of merely telling you what to do, this book will explain the approaches with practical self-tests based on modern science that probe your emotional depth.

The Stoics emphasizes reason as the primary basis for human conduct. Standing in sharp contrast with its major competitors: Plato emphasizes emotion (especially love), most clearly embodied by his idea of eros and Aristotle's theory that virtue is based upon habituation to perform all actions well. Stoics defined virtue itself not by external conquests or material accomplishments but instead as a state internal to the person which can be attained through practical wisdom, leading an ethical life, self

Take time for yourself. The ancient Greeks called it moral philosophy, the study of how to live according to reason. Nowadays, we say the word 'Stoic' has lost its meaning: Stoicism is about strength and endurance in the face of life's many problems. This compact guide lays out some observations on how a person can let go and eliminate negative emotions that keep us locked into unhappiness and fear by using remarkable techniques drawn from Marcus Aurelius, Seneca & other famous writers from this school of thought.

Marcus Aurelius was an emperor of Rome and a Stoic philosopher. His book Meditations is one of the most influential texts on Stoicism ever written. In it, he advises against responding to anger with more anger - "If you are angry, be assured that the thing which made you angry will not make you less so." Instead, Marcus Aurelius recommends practicing compassion for those who wronged us: "To feel no ill will toward them but only towards ourselves for being so stupid as to require what we do not need."

This advice can seem like a strange doctrine at first glance because many psychological models would recommend taking time away from our problems or resolving them through confrontation. However, when we practice mindfulness and cultivate self-compassion rather than judging ourselves harshly and making unfavorable comparisons between ourselves and others in order to justify our feelings of anger, we can achieve true happiness despite

Additionally, trying other alternatives to regulate anger has been proven to be very beneficial, as well as the key to any Stoic principle is to regulate your emotions. For example, you can use Mental Distancing.

It is a technique you can use to help yourself calm down when you are experiencing anger. It is a coping skill that many psychologists recommend as an alternative to suppressing your feelings or lashing out at the source of displeasure, which in turn may lead to negative consequences like regret and long-term damage.

Mental distancing involves mentally putting physical distance between yourself and the object of your anger, giving yourself a momentary respite from feeling angry by removing it from your presence for the time being.

Try these steps:

- Take three deep breaths, focusing on breathing in through your nose and out through pursed lips;
- Picture something that brings you joy - this is not necessarily something visible but could be anything like listening to a favorite song or reading one of your favorite books; 3) When you feel calmer, picture whatever caused you to anger again while

Another way to regulate internal emotions is to learn not to obsess about elements outside of our control. Remind yourself that there are things in your life that you can and cannot have jurisdiction over; For example, a person's height, the color of their eyes, voice, and much more. Meditation can prove to be a useful tool when it comes to practices like these.

Virtues of Stoicism

The Stoic virtues "are action-guiding dispositions," which are defined as moral excellence seen as a form of knowledge.

The cardinal virtues of Stoicism are wisdom, justice, courage, and temperance. This style of philosophy was invented by the philosopher Zeno. He believed that people should focus on what they can control and not get too caught up in things outside their control. For example, suppose someone has a disability. In that case, they cannot change, like being paralyzed or having autism- then it is better to accept this condition instead of feeling sorry for themselves. The Stoics also believe that our knowledge is limited, and we should avoid making judgments about things we do not know for sure, which leads us into error when forming opinions. A person would be considered wise if they had attained an understanding of the truth and could teach others to attain this understanding so they might live a life without disturbance.

Greek philosophers of the early Roman Empire, such as Cicero, Seneca, and Plutarch, distinguished the cardinal or primary virtues and the derived secondary virtues. As explained below, there are four primary Stoic virtues: wisdom (or insight), courage, self-control (also called continence), and justice, while other sources add piety to these lists.

In essence, wisdom merely is understanding the way things are or can grasp it. The wise person understands what he/she truly values and knows how to act in accordance with this knowledge. A person who is not aware of what is essential will have a much more difficult time realizing life's necessities.

Cardinal Virtues of Stoicism is the part of ancient philosophy that brought to existence: a newer psychotherapy form based on principles that people still use today. When statesmen like Marcus Aurelius went through difficult times—some lasting for months, even years at a time — he turned to these approaches as ways towards inspiring him towards living ethically

The Cardinal Virtues of Stoicism are:

- Practical Wisdom
- Justice
- Moderation
- Courage

Stoics, however, believe that the universe functions according to reason and logic, much like how an animal's body may be able to sense something instinctively long before our conscious mind has any idea what it might be sensing. Stoics' goal is not set on reacting to every opportunity, but working towards becoming more logical oneself. If we work toward being thoughtful, reasonable, and understanding humans, we can avoid suffering.

Philosophers have given many theories on what the universe is made up of. Plato was one of the first philosophers who studied the universe extensively, and he had a theory that there were five elements: fire, earth, air, water, and ether. He believed they were in perfect harmony with each other and that all things in this world are composed of these five elements. These days, scientists still investigate atoms that they believe make up everything we see around us and those inside us like our organs. The atom is so small that humans cannot know anything about them, but some scientists think they might exist because their equations show something should be out there, making up the mass of stuff in existence (things you can weigh). What do you think? Do you agree or disagree with any of these views?

The Stoic Happiness Triangle

We all know how to be happy. We have been conditioned from birth with the knowledge that happiness is something everyone wants- it is an intrinsic human desire and a fundamental part of life. However, what may not be as apparent are the steps one must take to achieve this goal. The Stoic Triangle of Happiness holds the key to a good, happy life by cultivating an excellent mental state. First things first: acknowledging what makes us unhappy and avoiding these things can help create lasting happiness.

Secondly, we need to practice mindfulness; living in the present moment without judgment or criticism of ourselves or others will allow us to sense more fulfillment in our lives. Lastly, you should develop your emotional resilience by cultivating positive thoughts about yourself and others while remaining calm during adversity.

The Stoic Triangle of Happiness holds the key for achieving long-lasting happiness through practicing mindfulness awareness and developing emotional resilience.

The Stoic Happiness Triangle, also known as the Trichotomy of Control, is a model created by Dr. David Meyers to describe the three types of happiness available for people and how they affect each other. Stoics' first type of happiness is valued as it does not require much and can be found in everyday life.

This type of happiness is called "eudaimonia," which means "having a good spirit." It arises from experiencing strong relationships with family or friends, and feeling like one's work makes them feel proud or useful and satisfied with what one has accomplished in their lives so far. People who have this form of happiness enjoy laughing at jokes with friends or getting excited about going on vacation. The second type of happiness is based solely on external factors, such as things we own or physical pleasures we experience.

A person can find happiness in their everyday life if they follow the Stoic Happiness Triangle. It consists of three points, namely virtue, friends, and pleasure. The first point is a virtue because it is a requirement for achieving the other two points. Friends are required for both joy and contentment as it aids self-sufficiency (which, according to Aristotle, is an essential aspect of a happy life). Pleasure provides the last point in this triangle because, without it, one cannot feel alive or experience joy from anything else; furthermore, after experiencing pain or suffering, one needs pleasurable experiences to remember what being well again feels.

Marcus Epictetus

Chapter 3: Principles of Stoicism

Philosophical principles are like the pillars that uphold society. These foundational concepts, such as free will, help people make sense of their lives and offer guidance for how to behave in specific situations.

It is a discipline that has been around for centuries. Simply put, philosophy asks what makes life worth living. What does it mean to be human? What are the essential values in our society, and how should we live? These are all questions that philosophers have pondered over hundreds of years. It is an exciting subject for people to study because it helps them think about what the world is like today and how they can change things like social norms or beliefs. Philosophy also teaches students critical thinking skills, which will help them in college and their future careers. They also learn the importance of asking the right questions to get answers, which prepares them for different kinds of interviews or job opportunities.

Philosophy does not just ask abstract questions but instead provides students with tools necessary to lead fulfilling lives full of meaning.

Stoicism's principles are a set of guidelines for life that can help people live better and more calmly. The key idea is that by accepting what happens, we free ourselves from the pain of excessive emotional reactions. When we stop struggling against things outside our control, it becomes easier to focus on what is in our power and take appropriate action. It also helps us avoid past mistakes and loss because these things happen regardless of the reaction we have towards them.

Philosophy without principles will not yield the best results. All you need to do is look at any ancient culture or civilization. You will see a set of fundamental beliefs, values, and practices that make up the community's foundation for its identity, its meaning, and its reason for being. If we don't have a firm grasp on this philosophy, then no matter what decisions we make, they will be in vain because they are not anchored in anything meaningful.

This philosophy also teaches us how to accept circumstances and make the best out of everything. When unfortunate things happen in life, they can be dealt with instead of dwelling on them. Stoics believe that this will help everyone live a more contented life. For example, if we did not have Stoicism's principles when practicing this philosophy, many of our learnings would be naught. It gives us the ability to know that we could have done something about a circumstance but chose not to do so just because we were too complacent or lazy to do what was necessary.

There are many principles in philosophy, and they all create structure. They are a guideline for how we live our lives, whom we spend time with, and how we should act towards others. The most important principle is the Golden Rule

This principle states that we should treat others as we would want to be treated ourselves. The best way to do this is to imagine what it would be like if someone else were in our situation and acted accordingly. For example, if you drive a car and see an old lady on the street looking lost, the right thing to do would be to stop your car and ask her for directions.

On the other hand, Stoicism is an ancient Greek philosophy that teaches people to be content and not worry about things outside of their control. It focuses on self-control, discipline, and reason as a means of overcoming destructive emotions. A person can practice Stoicism by following these four principles:

- Focus on your virtue
- Keep in mind that anything that happens, you do not have complete control over it
- Reason instead of emotionally; use logic to make decisions rather than being driven by fear or desire
- When something out of your control happens, accept it without complaint

In this philosophy, the good is defined as "what is complete according to nature for a rational being." For example, to be virtuous, one should do what they have been instructed by natural law and follow their true desires. The Stoics believe that happiness belongs only to wise people, and that misfortune comes from irrationality or wrongdoing. This was why Marcus Aurelius wrote his book Meditations: so he could remind himself everyday of how important it was for him to stay truthful with himself.

This philosophy breaks down the concept of virtue, dividing it into four main types: *wisdom, justice, courage, and moderation*. They believed that the virtuous life's goal is to agree with nature and realize that achieving this goal would be difficult for humans to do. In order to make it more attainable, they established three levels of virtue, which are that the person should pursue virtue as far as possible in their present circumstances. If one cannot pursue any further, they should follow their natural inclinations but not go beyond them. If still unable to achieve true happiness, they must avoid great vices such as desire or fear; this level is called "Inner Peace."

Wisdom

The Stoics have always prized wisdom. Zeno understood that there are many situations where talking is necessary to make an impression on people or win an argument. As such, he encouraged his followers to be active when it was appropriate but advised against excessiveness in communication; they should speak up only when needed and not waste time conversing just for the sake of being social.

Wisdom is an area of philosophy that deals with a person's understanding and usage of knowledge. It has been granted as one of the most critical topics in philosophical discourse for centuries. Philosophers often focus on different aspects such as its nature, wisdom's value, and what it means to be wise. One of Stoicism's essential virtues is wisdom; however, there are many different types and levels, such as practical knowledge. Wisdom in Stoicism is described as an individual's ability to understand the world, life, and their own emotions. It encompasses a moral understanding and insight. One way of gaining this virtue is by studying this philosophy intensely. This can help us cultivate our mindsets for better living and for making wiser decisions.

When we have wisdom, we can make fair use of what fate gives us because it enables us to look beyond current circumstances into the future, hoping that things will get better or at least change to be more tolerable. The other important aspect of being wise is realizing when it is time to stop fighting against fate and instead of surrendering oneself so that one can live harmoniously within its terms without struggling against them anymore. It is a disposition to be fair and virtuous, which will guide people in how they live their lives. By studying more in-depth about this philosophy, one can gain wisdom about oneself and learn more about becoming a better person.

The word phronêsis is translated from the Greek word φρόνησις, which literally means "wisdom." It was not the same as intelligence in ancient times because it dealt with moral and practical issues rather than abstract concepts. In Stoicism, phronêsis can be understood to mean practical wisdom or prudence.

For example, Marcus Aurelius writes: "No man will ever be called wise who conforms his actions to what he thinks right without considering what he considers possible; for such a person would never have done anything worthy of praise."

Justice

Philosophy is a field of intellectual inquiry that asks questions on the fundamental nature of being, existence, or reality. It is about asking big questions like what does justice mean, and how do we balance our own needs with others?

The first question would be who decides what justice is in the world? This answer can vary from person to person. For example, some people feel that the death sentence has already served true justice, while other people may believe that there are certain crimes where death might not be enough punishment for an individual. These arguments are often seen when discussing capital punishment and life imprisonment versus long-term sentences for those convicted of murder or other serious crimes. Different philosophers have different opinions on this topic, making it difficult to say whether they agree or disagree because their views vary so much!

Stoics subscribe to an idea that all material things in life are transient, temporary, and should not be pursued with any attachment. But what about justice? What does it mean for a stoic to pursue justice? Concentric circles are one way we can understand how this might work. A concentric circle comprises two circles drawn on top of each other called "bands."

There will be different levels or degrees in these bands on which people live their lives, from very low-to-lowest, from high-to-very highest. The goal for the true stoic philosopher would then be to move toward the center where he or she is most at peace with themselves and can dispassionately observe those who reside outside his inner

The concept of Justice in Stoicism is not entirely the same as the modern justice system in our legal systems. The Stoics think of it more like having a better moral compass or treating others fairly and doing what is right. This is seen as a virtue and one that we should practice in our day-to-day lives.

The idea comes from Aristotle's concept of "social justice," which means everyone has an equal opportunity to pursue happiness under social equality conditions, so there is no need for revolution or rebellion. On the other hand, for Plato, justice was more about what is just rather than moral: it refers to when people get what they deserve based on their actions and not their status (unless you are born into aristocracy).

Marcus Aurelius's description of justice is not the typical notion that we are exposed to in today's society. He defines it as "doing what you love and making sure that others can do what they love." They believe this is a correct representation of justice because it considers people happy rather than an imbalance between rich and poor.

The Sophists took a different approach with their idea of justice, which was merely giving people what they deserve. If they work hard for something, they should be rewarded for it, but also, if someone steals or kills, those actions should have repercussions. These two perspectives on justice show how vastly different these philosophers were from one another despite living around the same period.

Courage

There are different stances on what courage means and how it applies to the world. Some argue that courage is not an instinct but a conscious decision to take risks to be successful, while others see courage as a way of being in the present moment. The philosopher who wrote most about this was Aristotle; he believed that there were many bravery forms, including physical, intellectual, moral, and social.

Being courageous in Stoicism is crucial. It can open your mind to new possibilities, make you feel more confident and happier, and even be a lifesaver! You might have heard of how courage helped the protagonist survive Pearl Harbor's attack during World War II. However, did you know that it also led to life-saving discoveries like penicillin? All because one brave scientist dared to defy orders from her boss and test out a potentially risky hypothesis! If only she had been afraid of failing.

Marcus Aurelius was a Roman Emperor who was also broadly known for his contribution to stoicism. He famously once said, "All you need is enough. It is good or bad, scary, or exciting. A man must live in the present and face it with courage." This quote has resonated with many throughout history as they have found strength in this wisdom when faced with life's challenges.

In stoicism, Courage is the ability to exert one's will in the face of risk. This Virtue can be seen as a type of bravery, and brave people are admired for their strength to do what others may not have done before them because they were too scared or nervous. It takes courage to fight a battle even if there is an 80% chance you will lose because that means you're willing to take risks other people would not dare go near, but that also means you stand more than just a 20% chance at winning! Stoics believe that bravery is an essential virtue because it allows us to be courageous in difficult times. When we are courageous, we feel self-confidence and self-esteem boost up as well.

The Greek philosopher Epictetus believed that fear was something we could not control, but we could control our response to it. He came up with the idea of "premeditation" – a way of preparing for possible future events by visualizing them happening in your head. This is also known as Visual Imagery Therapy (VIT) and can help you feel more prepared when bad things happen.

Epictetus believed that people experience fear when they have a goal that is not totally under their control. If they change this to an internal one, then the feeling of terror will subside, and they will be able to make their move. For example, if someone played in a team sport and wanted to score a goal but did not know how or if it would work out, they might feel afraid. However, instead of making the external goal on behalf of oneself or others, he changes his priorities. Changing others' lives to just being happy with himself internally than the feelings of fear would subside he could live life without anxiety.

Moderation

The word "moderation" originated from the Latin word moderatio, which means to balance or equipoise. The ancient Greek school of Stoicism equates moderation with living in agreement with nature. To live according to our human nature and therefore within reason is to be moderate. We must exercise this virtue daily to not fall victim to natural desires such as sex, food, drink, and wealth.

Most philosophers have some moderation opinions. Those who believe in moderation's virtue think it is better to avoid extremes and go for a middle ground. They see it as a crucial part of life and say that everything would be chaotic without moderation. Many people in favor of such a philosophy might believe that extremism can sometimes be useful if done correctly and can lead to discoveries or success (or failure).

Socrates had a famous quote that, "The unexamined life is not worth living." He believed that the only way to live a meaningful life was by continuously questioning oneself. This concept would later be brought up in Stoicism and used as one of its fundamental philosophies. Sôphrosunê in Stoicism refers to tranquility, moderation, and self-control. It can also refer to wisdom and knowledge about what should or should not be done in different circumstances are essential traits for someone who has sôphrosunê.

Stoic philosophers viewed this virtue as being related to courage because it involves accepting any event which happens while maintaining mental calmness so that reason can prevail over emotion. They felt it necessary for people to have sôphrosynê because they considered all external influences uncontrollable: events happen whether we like them or not, but reasoned responses allow us.

The stoic doctrine was that virtue, the only good, consists of a will that follows reason; happiness follows virtue and should not be pursued as an end for itself or externally. Stoics are united to other philosophers because they believe that external goods like health, wealth, position, etc., are necessary but not sufficient for living well.

In defense of moderation in Stoicism, Stoics argue that the concept is not about practicing complete abstinence from worldly pleasures. Instead, it can be argued that ancient Stoics believed that it was essential to practice moderating one's desires and impulses so as to live a life of tranquility without being hampered by external circumstances. They believed this especially included exercising restraint with regards to material goods such as food and drink, but also things like anger or lustful thoughts. This allowed one to have a fulfilling life while still experiencing these pleasures when appropriate.

Voluntary Choices

Instead of being pushed into it by external forces, the idea of choosing on your own is integral to free will. Philosophers have debated the extent to which our choices are voluntary or not for centuries. The most influential philosopher in this debate was probably Jean-Paul Sartre. He argued that since factors outside ourselves determine all actions, we cannot make any authentic choices. Instead, he said that choice is an illusion because everything we do is just something that happens either due to internal psychological, or external environmental circumstances.

Epictetus's teachings are still popular today because they offer practical lessons for living in challenging situations. For example, when faced with hardship or danger, he advises to "bear what is necessary" without complaint and focus on long-term goals instead of short-term discomfort. Stoicism's fundamental principle is that there are some things we can control and others we cannot; it is essential to use our judgment wisely so that we do not waste time on matters outside our power. He uses analogies from nature to illustrate how life unfolds over time: "You may break an urn, but you will never break its seal." This means that even if something terrible happens now or in the future, it cannot erase all past happiness.

A Stoic's decision-making algorithm is simple. It is based on the idea of "living with respect to Nature." This means that one should live according to what they have been given at birth and bring out their full potential by behaving virtuously and doing good things for others. It also means having a calm demeanor and not being carried away by external events or other people's actions. This philosophy's goal was to teach people how to control themselves to be happy even if outside circumstances are terrible.

A Stoic has a set of beliefs that are different from those in mainstream society. They believe that all people have the same potential and should be treated equally, regardless of their status in life or wealth. Zeno first introduced this idea when he initially created the school for philosophers and named it The Stoa Poikile (or only "The Porch"). On this porch, the philosophers believed it was essential to remain focused on what they could control instead of worrying about things outside their sphere of influence.

This Hellenistic philosophy values self-control and having a proper focus on one's choices. In Stoicism, the individual controls their desires to maintain emotional stability and happiness, which leads to overall well-being.

They even go so far as to say that they should live with pain or poverty without complaining because it does not hurt anyone. The doctrine of personal ethics in this philosophy states that we are not slaves to our emotions but instead masters of them.

Chapter 4: Psychological Resilience

Psychological Resilience is the ability to get through an emotional crisis and return to pre-crisis status quickly. This form of mental prowess can be developed in numerous ways, including meditation and self-talk exercises. It is vital for people from all walks of life, but especially those who have anxiety and depression due to high-stress levels in their daily lives. Psychologists identify two types of psychosocial resilience, positive and negative, both of which are important to the therapeutic process.

Positive psychosocial resilience refers to an individual's ability to resist stressors in their environment that could cause mental health issues such as PTSD or clinical depression. Negative psychosocial resilience is not so much the avoidance of stress but rather how a person manages it when it arises. The three primary skills for managing anxiety and reducing its intensity are self-soothing, control mastery, and distraction from worrying thoughts."

The Stoics believed that the best way to overcome negative emotions was to face them. To do this, they engaged in a technique called "negative visualization," where they imagined worst-case scenarios (losing their job or health). This helped strengthen their resilience and prevented them from giving up during difficult times. As part of a practice known as "premeditatio malorum" the Stoic would also re-live past tragedies by visualizing each painful event in vivid detail. These practices have been shown to help people better handle emotional problems like anxiety and depression over time. The idea of premeditatio malorum is used in Stoicism to indicate that a person should contemplate the worst possible outcome for any situation. For example, if someone were considering taking out an insurance plan, they would need to know the costs and all potential scenarios where they might need it- even unlikely ones. This way, when they experience something good or bad that was not planned for at first, it is not so shocking and can be dealt with more calmly.

To become mentally healthy in Stoicism, the first thing to do is challenge your preconceptions about life and death.

It's much more than just a philosophical exercise. To be happy, you need to think differently from how society pressures you to act. You need to question yourself: Is my suffering necessary? What will happen if I die tomorrow? Am I living as an honest human being?

The second thing is that all external events are indifferent because they don't have any causal link with our mental state. For example, whether someone says something nice or mean or praised or criticized does not affect us internally, whatever happens externally. The third thing is that there are no right or wrong things but only thoughts of value judgments, which can vary depending on time and place but not on who judges them- ourselves, other people, etc.-

Epictetus helped modify the philosophy in order to make it more practical. One of his significant contributions was the introduction of "reserve clauses." These are specific phrases or arguments that we use in our thinking when we are dealing with intense emotions. They allow us to think about a situation while still feeling passion for it, but they remove some intensity to act rationally and logically. Reserve clauses also help us improve our ability to judge things objectively because they cause us to pause every few moments during these thoughts and consider something else from another perspective before continuing with them.

The reserve clause shows that a person's thoughts and actions can change their fate. The Stoic philosopher Epictetus called it "hupexhairesis." This word originates from the Greek prefix "hupo," which means "under," and the verb "exairein," meaning "to choose." It is the right word to know if you want to be stoic.

"God willing..." or "Fate permitting..." is a statement that explains the reserve clause. These statements acknowledge that at least part of the outcome is not under their control. Additionally, this aspect acknowledges some doubt about the success of whatever endeavor they are speaking about and taking responsibility for any possible failures of said endeavors.

A person may use this phrase when trying to discourage other people from participating in something risky or challenging because there is a sense that failure will happen if it has not already happened previously. The person could be using this as a way to cover themselves from criticism should anything go wrong or acknowledge possible past mistakes caused by them, which say: "I was warned before, but I did it anyway."

Perspective

This is an important concept that has been debated by scholars for centuries. The argument can be summarized as follows: either the world we experience and perceive is all there is, or other realities exist apart from our perceptions. This debate revolves around two schools of thought- the school of Epicureanism and the School of Plato.

Modern-day philosophers have always been interested in how people see things. It is the backbone of many philosophies. Perspective is a concept that has been around for centuries, and philosophers from Plato to Nietzsche have written about it extensively. Recently, there have been modern psychologists who think they know the answer to what perspective truly means. However, philosophers still debate this topic fiercely at conferences and online forums where those with academic credentials can get together and share their thoughts on the subject as peers."

On the other hand, however., it is a quintessential part of Stoicism because it allows you to see a bigger picture and find your inner peace. Using perspective, one can avoid being bogged down by the little things in life that do not matter, like what others think or how they judge themselves. Perspective also allows for a sense of control over any situation. Taking everything in stride and not being so reactive is a crucial part of stoic philosophy and compassion towards oneself and others.

This philosophy aims for self-mastery, calmness in the face of adversity, and good moral character—being reactive means being emotionally swayed by external events (like jealousy or anger), which defeats the purpose of its principles. The philosophy strives to be more reflective and less emotional. According to Stoicism's guiding principle, this ability to control emotions through reflection makes it easier for one to lead a virtuous life.

Proudly adhering to this philosophy is difficult for some people today because we are continually being fed messages telling us our lives are out of our control. This kind of thinking is supported by everything from the news cycle to social media, where we can feel like there is nothing good happening anywhere in the world at any time. However, suppose you have given yourself a chance for long enough to get your bearings. In that case, you will realize that perspective is not just about seeing things as they are — it means seeing them all together and understanding their place one within another.

The School of Plato & Epicureanism

Epicureanism believes that who holds to what is termed "localism" (the belief above that everything exists here). Epicurus founded this school of philosophy. The theory's central idea is that happiness, or pleasure, is the most important intrinsic good and should be pursued in life.

They believe that one's happiness should not conversely depend on external circumstances but on what happens in one's mind. They also hold to the belief of localism, which states that all things are made up of atoms and voids and nothing else; this means they do not believe anything can come from nothing at all. The atomic makeup makes everything uniform because what we see around us are just aggregations of atoms with no outside influence (Mcgrath).

Plato was a philosopher from the Classical era of ancient Greece, famous for his teachings on justice. He was well known for his work "The Republic," which discusses many points about what constitutes a good government and society. It also includes an example of Platonic philosophy, which explores the idea that knowledge is not absolute but can be divided into lower forms, such as perception, opinion, and belief. The school of Plato believed, which upholds a more dualistic understanding known as "pluralism" (the idea that things happen not only here but also elsewhere).

This teaching goes against some primary schools in academia at the time, such as Aristotelianism. A school that argued that there were various levels or degrees to the knowledge should be pursued to understand.

Regarding pluralism, this school says that when building a democracy, different groups with diverse interests need to be considered if they all want their voices heard equally on matters affecting them. For example, people who wish for less government control may have more influence over social policy.

On the other hand, the Stoics agreed with pluralism because they believed that it was possible to know both worlds through prayerful reflection and contemplation. They saw these parallel realities as existing outside time and space, where one could explore them without being subjected to anything.

Stoicism and Pluralism are two philosophies that both have an emphasis on the individual. This philosophy describes "a system which teaches man how he can become happy and secure." It was initially intended to be taught only to members of the upper class who were expected to govern others.

One significant difference between Stoics and Pluralists is that while the former usually sees himself as a citizen of one state, among others, the latter believes in universal citizenship. A stoic either accepts or rejects the social change, whereas pluralists believe that it happens gradually over time - though they also acknowledge its importance for society's well-being.

Both philosophies take different government approaches; where stoics believe in letting natural law regulate society without interference from human beings, Pluralism recognizes humans' need.

Strengthening Oneself

What do philosophers think about strengthening oneself mentally? Some say that it is a waste of time, some argue for it, and others say that there is no point in the first place. It largely depends on what kind of philosophy you adhere to!

Stoicism is a philosophy that aims to live life without limits or regrets by living according to nature and its laws rather than changing them for their desires. In ancient Greece, there was a group called Cynic philosophers who encouraged emotional resilience through indifference or apathy towards pleasure or pain.

Also, lack of fear about death; while doing good deeds regardless of the outcome is positive or negative; and practicing self-control when faced with anger, grief, jealousy, or lust.

Cynics have been making waves in the philosophical world as of late. They generally believe that "the good life is one without illusions" and strive for an appropriately difficult existence to make sure they never get too comfortable with their lives. This attitude has led them to be labeled as pessimistic philosophers who suffer emotional resilience and often lead a solitary existence. People view this philosophy negatively because they seem incapable of being happy or satisfied with what they have.

However, this philosophy provides people with freedom from passions that could distract them from true happiness. They also teach people how to live well without relying on external goods like wealth or health; instead, it focuses on cultivating knowledge, virtue, friendship, and the right action to live happily—at the same time, acknowledging that we will die someday.

The difference between Cynics and Stoics is that the former believes the world to be evil while the latter thinks it to be indifferent. This significant disagreement in ancient philosophy sets the two apart. Nevertheless, they both have similar views on approaching their lives. The Stoics were ascetics who believed that happiness is not found in material goods or outside events but rather through virtue. They also believed that there is nothing wrong with pleasure as long as it does not get in the way of one's pursuit of wisdom and courage. Apart from all that, they thought that people should focus on what can be controlled (such as actions). This practice entails that we should not worry about fate or other people's opinions because it is beyond our control.

Unlike Stoicism, Cynicism focuses more heavily on nature and living according to natural principles, which ultimately means embracing life by feeling all its joys and pains entirely without trying to avoid them

Understanding your emotions when practicing stoicism can also help you progress through life better. It is vital to learn how to redirect your emotions. A practice we have talked about before in this book is negative visualization. This technique involves imagining what would happen if you lost all your current possessions and status in life. This practice can significantly build resilience and help you enjoy what you have now better because it builds the idea of "there will always be someone different, for better or worse."

This philosophy stems from the idea that all human ills come from an incorrect understanding of what the world is and how we should behave in it. One element within Stoicism is called "reserve," or self-control, which teaches people to redirect their emotions in the right way without hurting someone else's feelings. It is quintessential to have growth without thwarting someone else's emotional progress. That is something that goes against Stoic principles and will not bring forward good results.

Stoicism's founders believed that people should be guided solely by their reason and not emotions like anger or love. In essence, stoics are taught how they should live according to their world without affecting them. This practice is done through moral reasoning and understanding what makes up their willpower, called "prohairesis" (Plato).

Chapter 5: Modern Day Practices

Modern-day stoicism does exist. It is still a practical philosophy that teaches its followers to ignore pain, avoid emotional reactions, and maintain calm in dangerous or stressful situations. It originated in Ancient Greece during the 4th century BC and was followed by many of history's greatest thinkers.

It is still a philosophy that teaches one to practice restraint and be content with what they have. Stoics believe that happiness resides in your mind, not the circumstances of life, and can be achieved by practicing restraint or virtue. It was an ancient Greek word meaning "to keep oneself from being disturbed."

An exciting example of this dynamic at work is when Epictetus says, "Don't outsource your happiness," as he encouraged his students to take charge of their beliefs and emotions rather than outsourcing these things to external factors as society or success. This idea may seem contradictory, but this philosophy is all about balancing different aspects within yourself, so you don't always feel like a pendulum swinging between extremes; experiencing both joys along with challenges just means you're living well!

Practitioners believe it can help them remain steadfast even when faced with difficult circumstances like poverty or war because stoics do not let emotions get the best of them. Stoic philosophers such as Seneca have said that we should be detached from our desires to control our thoughts, which leads to feelings of anger and sadness. (There are many ways for people to practice modern-day stoicism with one being through careful introspection)

The philosophy of Stoicism is very different in the current age. In the past, stoic philosophers were able to teach their philosophies without fear of backlash or attack from other religions. Today's society is much more interconnected and interdependent on one another, which can lead to less tolerance for new ideas that go against what people consider "normal."

Additionally, there are many misconceptions about how Stoicism should be practiced to live a happy life. The popular idea seems to be that it consists mainly of suppressing any emotion or thought that would cause unhappiness, yet this leaves room for negative emotions like anger and envy. Those have been deemed necessary by individual modern thinkers (ex: Freud). The modern-day practice talks a lot more about not thinking about anything wrong happening at all, but again this leaves room for imagining bad things and trying not to think about them.

Before we go any further into the philosophy, let us first discuss a few applicable modern-day practices.

Contemplating your Mortality

Philosophers have been tackling the subject of mortality for as long as we can remember. One of the earliest philosophical questions about death was posed by Socrates, who asked, "What is the fear of death?" (Nussbaum). The Greeks talked a lot about death, but it was not until one particular philosopher that we began to question what exactly happens after you die; Nicomachean Ethics by Aristotle. He describes how there are two types of infinity: temporal and spatial. When you

Stoic Meditations

die, your time on earth ceases to exist, and therefore, your life in this world also comes to an end once death occurs and leaves only memories in our minds forever.

Stoicism provides guidelines for living an ethical life. It does this by analyzing the sources of good and evil in the world to determine how people should act. In other words, Stoicism helps us know what we should do with our lives if we want to live wisely and virtuously. One crucial question is whether humans can be virtuous without God; after all, according to Christianity and Islam, there are moral absolutes that cannot be questioned. The Stoics said no - even though they left open the possibility that events may have happened differently than they did historically. "If God had not created everything as he did," wrote Marcus Aurelius in Meditations, "someone else would have created something different."

Amor fati is a stoic practice worth noting here: it involves accepting one's fate and understanding the depth of mortality. Furthermore, it means to be willing to love your destiny, whatever it may be. Some people use this as an analogy to accept death and pain in life; they believe that they will have a more fulfilling life by embracing their fate because they will appreciate every moment more. However, not all stoics practiced Amor fati - some thought that living well was their main priority and only if you had lived well can your welcome death

Stoicism is an ancient philosophical tradition and way of living where the philosophers believed that death is not something to be feared but rather the natural conclusion of life. Stoics regard the universe as a large machine in which humans play a small part; they think it has no concern for them, so they do not need to fear death. To them, the idea of dying is merely a necessary aspect of life and should not be feared because all things must come to an end eventually. This aspect teaches its practitioners to live without any desire or emotion interfering with their judgment.

Cultivating Philanthropy

Achieving philanthropy in Stoicism is something that requires a lot of self-examination and reflection. One should first contemplate their own emotions and the role they have in others' lives. Stoics believe that living life with virtue provides the best path to happiness. This aspect entails being kind, thoughtful, generous, and tolerant - all without expecting anything in return."

Stoicism is a philosophy that involves self-examination. The goal of self-examination is to keep us in line with virtue and not let our emotions get the best of us. It can be difficult for beginners to practice this when learning Stoicism because it requires being aware of your emotional standpoints, feelings, and reactions. When practicing self-examinations, you should be mindful that there are two types. One type of practice occurs after something happens (anticipatory) and the other during an event or activity (real-time). Asking yourself questions such as "am I acting out my own will?" or "whom am I becoming?" during these sessions can help you evaluate if you have been living according to virtue lately.

Self-examinations are essential because they can teach us how to control and redirect our emotions and impulses, which is an indispensable part of a stoic lifestyle. It also helps in developing self-awareness, another critical component of the practice. Self-examinations should be practiced at least once every day to ensure that we live according to the core principles that define this way of life. Doing so will help maintain a clear conscience and positive outlook on life.

Self-Retreat

A self-retreat is a personal journey of introspection and reflection. Stoicism, one of the earliest Greek philosophies, emphasizes the importance of living according to nature. The self-retreat enables an individual to live following their human nature rather than being governed by external forces. This practice can also be done alone at home or as part of a group excursion led by a guide who provides instruction and guidance during the process.

This practice has been around for quite some time, and it is a popular trend and an ancient practice. Some people say that they need to take the time away from the world to gain clarity on their lives. This practice can be done by physically secluding themselves or mentally through meditation, contemplation, or prayer.

One of the best ways to practice self-retreat is to isolate yourself from other people and work on your thoughts. This practice allows you to give yourself time for introspection, leading to a more peaceful state of mind if you are not content with where you are in life. Standard methods include meditation, reading, or writing as these pastimes allow one's mind to float away from reality into a world all their own.

If you are contemplating going out on an excursion for your self-retreat, then there are a few things you should keep in mind. You must make sure you are well-equipped for your self-retreat. Many things can go wrong if you don't plan accordingly - as such, here are a few common mistakes anone might end up making:

First and foremost, you should have a good idea of what you want out of the retreat before planning anything else. You might want to create some goals or set some parameters to know what your focus will be. Doing this will help ensure that all of the time spent on the retreat is sustainable and meaningful; otherwise, there might not be any improvement!

Secondly, it's necessary to keep in mind who'll be able to check on your progress during the retreat. If nobody knows where you are or who can reach out, then there won't be anyone available who could offer assistance when needed most!

Maintaining a Journal

Journaling and Stoicism are both ancient practices with modern-day benefits. Journaling can help in practicing Stoic thought by recording emotions, feelings, or events throughout the day without attaching any judgments to these experiences. For example, if a person feels frustrated because they have been waiting for something too long, journaling about this experience could include writing 'I am annoyed right now' rather than 'This person is so inconsiderate.' This practice helps with resisting judgment of external situations and living a life following specific values and principles.

Stoic Meditations

A journal is a useful tool for self-reflection and self-growth. It is also an outlet for your thoughts, feelings, memories, dreams, and fears. Maintaining a journal lets you record what happened to you and how you reacted to the events. A philosopher could say that this is important because it will help with understanding ourselves better.

You can practice this by keeping a record of your thoughts by taking out a sheet of paper and simply writing down any question about the practice. Make the writing as detailed as possible, including where the idea came from or what exactly is bothering you. Once finished, choose how you want to answer that particular question; there are many different writing purposes in your journal: self-reflection, confessionals, knowledge retention, and more! You can use this time to say anything on your mind so long as it is not hurtful towards yourself or others. If you are not aware about where to start with a new concern, then focus on one of these four areas: physical/external condition (your body), mental state (thoughts), social interactions (relationships), external events (circumstances).

Practicing Mindfulness

What is practicing mindfulness in Stoicism? It means living in the present moment, non-judgmentally and without anxiety. This practice aims to cultivate a sense of tranquility by focusing on what you can control and not on things outside your sphere of influence. This technique also helps to decrease negative emotions like anger, resentment, regret, or guilt.

One of the main goals of Stoicism is the practice of focus and mindfulness. Practitioners learn to eliminate unhealthy emotions such as anger or anxiety, which will be replaced with positive feelings like tranquility, happiness, and courage. Although Stoics do not need a god figure to feel at peace with themselves because they are confident that all things happen by fate alone, this does not diminish their appreciation of nature's beauty. There is no one way to follow the philosophy: some believe in being self-sufficient while others say you should care about others but not too much not to allow them to affect your decisions.

Practicing mindfulness allows one to be more self-aware and mindful of their thoughts, feelings, surroundings, and actions. For example, if you were faced with a task such as cleaning out your closet, it would give you the time needed to complete other tasks. Life becomes less stressful overall when completing chores and completing them more efficiently than if they were rushed through quickly due to lack of concentration.

The state of zen, "a state of consciousness which people strive to attain through meditation and self-discipline," might not be achievable for most. However, practicing focus can help us develop our concentration to control what happens in our lives—instead of feeling like life controls us. Practicing focus helps overcome mental barriers, including depression or anxiety because it helps you see things differently. It also teaches discipline and patience, which will make you more successful at work and in your personal life because those skills often come into play.

One common enemy you will face in the modern-day when practicing Stoicism is Ego. This harmful sense of self-esteem slows us down and prevents us from reaching our full potential. It stops people from working towards their dreams, goals, and ambitions. When we are too concerned about what others think of us, we can't find the success that is ours to exploit.

The Stoics believed that getting in touch with one's emotions was detrimental to a person's well-being; instead, they advocated living a life void of emotional expression not to be swayed by external events or circumstances. Ego has no place in Stoicism because it inhibits personal development and growth, which eventually leads to feelings of inadequacy, low self-esteem, depression, etcetera

The benefits of practicing Stoicism in a regulated manner in the modern-day and age are numerous. Including greater self-control, improved mental health, increased productivity, and better relationships with others are only a few of the benefits. Reaching goals becomes more comfortable because you do not give up so easily on your desires when obstacles arise. Practicing Stoicism can also help people maintain a sense of equanimity during difficult times, which can be especially beneficial for those who live through traumatic events such as war or natural disasters.

Chapter 6: Meditation

Meditation is a self-help tool that can increase awareness of our thoughts, feelings, and emotions. Meditation can also help people with anxiety or chronic pain find relief from their symptoms.

More and more people are practicing mindfulness as a way to help them deal with stress. This technique is also being used in schools because it has been proven to help students concentrate better, learn more effectively, and behave well. Some people argue that this is not an effective form of meditation because you cannot focus on anything else but your breathing for practice duration. However, what if you have problems concentrating or focusing on anything else but your breathing? Mindful meditation can be helpful in those circumstances! Before accepting mindfulness, we need to ask ourselves how often I will use this technique outside my home or office to relax while sitting there meditating at work?

It is a notable practice that has been around for centuries as well. The practice can be done in several ways to help clear the mind, reduce stress, and promote general health. One standard method focuses on breathing (something we do naturally) or other repetitive thoughts such as counting your breath or reciting mantras or prayers. Meditation also helps with self-esteem issues by giving you time to think about what makes your life meaningful and how you want it to unfold.

This practice is an ancient tradition that has been practiced for centuries worldwide to give people a chance at peace of mind while also reducing stress levels and promoting general health. There are many different approaches to meditating - some more active than others - but generally, they involve focusing on either breathing (something we do without thought) or another repetitive activity like counting breaths.

Meditation can also be used to help find balance in life. This chapter will tell you why meditation can be useful and use it for the best results. Meditation has been present in many different cultures from ancient times until today, and now there are more benefits than ever before.

It is generally believed that meditation was introduced in the Buddhist tradition to help people with their physical, mental, and spiritual well-being. However, some scientists believe this may not be true because meditative practices have been documented all over Asia, Europe, and Africa since 5000 BC. There are many distinctions on what constitutes a "meditation," but one thing is exact: it all requires us to move beyond our everyday thoughts and worries that seem so important at first glance but are not worth our time or energy want peace of mind.

Stoicism and meditation have in common the idea of practicing how to be more aware. This practice can help people handle difficult situations better and learn from them, so they do not find themselves getting upset or angry about things they have no control over. Meditation helps develop self-control and emotional stability by helping you understand your feelings and thoughts on a deeper level.

Stoics believed true happiness was achieved by focusing on what can be controlled and not worrying about things outside our control like other people's behavior or natural disasters. A lot of which can be achieved by using meditation as a tool — this practice pairs fantastically with reflecting on oneself and spending time understanding the roots of their emotional conflicts.

Some people believe that self-control is the ability to resist urges and desires. The stoics, however, view it as one's ability to live in harmony with oneself. For example, drinking water when you are thirsty or eating a meal when you are hungry is seen as practicing self-control because they give your body what it needs. In contrast, eating ice cream (even though you're not hungry) shows a lack of self-control because it does not satisfy any physical need and will only result in regret afterward if consumed. Stoicism teaches that our emotions should be met with understanding rather than judgment to better control them - like anger, which can create violence or fear, which causes paralysis. This philosophy could also teach us how to manage emotions such as disappointment from failed attempts at achieving goals or sadness from the death of loved ones without being emotionally overwhelmed by these events.

Meditation, on the other hand, focuses on self-knowledge and mindfulness. Integrating this practice into a routine can be difficult for someone who practices Stoicism because it does not typically include meditation or contemplation as part of its teachings. However, some Stoic philosophers practice Zen Buddhism, which includes aspects of mediation in their spiritual practices.

Mindfulness meditation, however, is an essential and defining characteristic of Stoicism. However, it is less a contemplative and pragmatic activity than in other Eastern philosophies such as Buddhism. Buddhists would use mindfulness to detach themselves from the ego-driven self, whereas Stoics use it to build up their will power by observing sensations without judging them. When you meditate on pain, for example, you're supposed to see oneself as a dispassionate observer rather than someone who is being tormented. It might sound like some masochistic practice, but actually, this technique can be beneficial. For example, when we feel overwhelmed or powerless, understanding the goal ahead becomes essential. In this case, the goal is not about getting rid of all emotions but learning how to deal with them better and dissolve them.

Having the mindset that "a stoic does not need to learn about meditation." is natural. This practice might seem unnecessary because people might think that a stoic should attain clarity without meditation's emotional benefits and focus on the inner self. The truth is, most people are not natural-born stoics who can ignore pain or suffering. We all suffer from negative emotions like anger, depression, sadness, and fear; it is just part of being human. We must recognize these feelings so we do not feel crippled by them when they arise in our lives - which they will at some point! That is where meditation comes in. Meditation helps you build resilience against life's inevitable tragedies because understanding your mind better than anyone else does give you more control over how it responds to things that happen around you every day."

In Stoicism's early life, Zeno taught that philosophy could be used to find peace in one's mind. This state's pursuit is called "apatheia" or "a peaceful and stable condition of the soul." Achieving apatheia involves a skilled core to the Stoic philosophy: meditation. Meditation is an active practice where one trains oneself to focus on breathing or repeating sequential thoughts. By practicing mindfulness, we can control our mental processes and detach from any external disturbances. This practice allows us access into our minds without being pulled away by worldly worries such as money or relationship shortcomings. With these practices, we can learn how to balance out stressors better to achieve a well-tempered state of mind.

Stress can be a constant in anyone's life. It happens to everyone, and it cannot be entirely prevented. The more you try to avoid stressors, the more they will show up unexpectedly and catch you off guard.

A balance of positive thoughts and activities can help reduce your stress levels and respond calmly when a stressful event happens. When practicing stoicism with meditation, take several deep breaths before responding to calm down quickly or see the situation from a different perspective than what's causing your stress at that moment in time.

Stoic Philosophers believe that we need to find peace with what happens in life and understand the nature of cause and effect. The Stoics believed that your response to events determines your emotional well-being when you are faced with a stressful situation. It is not about the event itself but how we react to it. For example, if someone told you they hated your favorite TV show or something else personal to yourself, just refuse to let this information affect you. Rather than feeling hurt or upset over these types of life occurrences, stoic philosophy teaches us how to accept these things without judgment and learn from them when possible.

Stoics believe that to embrace the philosophy entirely, you must first come to terms with life. This practice entails that you should not be bothered by the opinions of other people. The philosophy focuses on understanding one's self better to achieve happiness through inner peace. The focus of meditation and clarity in this circumstance is more on what you can control instead of focusing on external factors.

Philosophers believe external circumstances cannot control human emotions and happiness, as they are under our power. Many people have utilized this theory and mixed in meditation to better their lives and become more grounded in reality.

Stoicism is essentially an affirmation technique to help you develop an awareness of your thoughts and feelings, allowing you to control them rather than be controlled by them. Stoics do this by accepting all things without exhibiting any outward emotion or reaction; instead, they focus on what they can change, such as their reactions or how to train themselves not to feel so strongly about the situation at hand. One would essentially use Stoic philosophy for cognitive behavioral therapy - but with self-awareness instead of others' insight (such as therapists).

Stoic exercises can include meditation, and some have been around for over 400 years. After all, stoicism is philosophy and school of thought, which states we should not let emotions or desires affect our decisions. They also offer the meditative discipline of apatheia as a way to separate oneself from emotion-inducing situations.

Apatheia, or "passionlessness." is a practice that helps a stoic avoid overthinking things. This exercise helps them not to lose control of their emotions, suppress any urges for pleasure or excitement (since they can quickly lead to trouble), and keep themselves from being angry at other people when it does not affect them.

A mindful meditation practice could offer some benefits from practicing stoicism while meditating by simultaneously calming your body and cultivating an attitude of gratitude for everything you have right now.

This form of stoic meditation is a practice that helps you focus on the present moment and be in tune with your emotions. It is a fantastic way to calm yourself down if you're feeling overwhelmed or stressed because it reminds you of what you can control at any given time and puts things into perspective for you. In order to start practicing Stoic mindfulness meditation, there are some steps to follow:

- Focus on one thing that's happening right now. This aspect could be something as simple as breathing or taking notice of your surroundings
- Incorporate the Four Disciplines: Control over how we react to events; Indifference about those events' outcomes; Focus on our own goals rather than worldly success; A sense of voluntary self-discipline

This philosophy is perfect for people who are tired of feeling stressed out as well. What makes this system so great is that it teaches how-to live-in harmony with all of life's inevitable conditions, making you feel better and more balanced than ever before.

Some ways that can help you practice this type of mindfulness include:

One meditative practice regularly would be using a timer or stopwatch and setting an ordinary task like washing dishes or cleaning your room. Inhale air into your lungs deeply while focusing on the present moment and exhale until there is no air left in you. Repeat emptying one's lungs as long as the timer goes off-focus on anything but what you are doing to stay focused throughout the process.

Mindful Meditation can be very beneficial. It can reduce stress and anxiety, which is shown to be useful for those with chronic pain. Additionally, Meditation has also been found to help with obesity-related problems in adults and children and improve a person's cardiovascular health. There are other psychological benefits, too, such as reducing depression or social phobia by working on one's self-image. Meditation has been shown to decrease anorexia nervosa symptoms and binge eating among obese individuals for those who suffer from eating disorders.

There are different types of meditation. "mindful" or "stoic" meditation is one of the many kinds of practices available for us. These meditations focus on the breath and help practitioners develop awareness by focusing the mind on the present moment instead of thinking about past or future events. It is believed to be more effective for relaxation than other meditation types, such as Transcendental Meditation or Zen Meditation. This type of mediation can be done during the day; it is typically practiced in the morning before doing anything else. It has also been shown to improve blood pressure, immune system function, and mood regulation with regular practice over an extended period.

Chapter 7: Becoming a Modern Stoic

Stoicism is a philosophy. It is all about staying calm in the face of adversity. The ancient Greeks had it right when they said, "suffer what must be suffered" and "bear ills as they arise." Sounds easy, I know, but even people like us who want to stay happy cannot always do so. We cannot control everything that happens on our path through life, and sometimes things happen. However, stoicism does not ask you not to have emotions; instead, it asks you to observe them without any improper insight.

In the twenty-first century, being stoic has taken on different meanings depending on whom you ask. In its most popular form, people have adopted this philosophy as self-help for modern living by creating their philosophies and implementing them into their lifestyles. For example, some modern stoics use Stoicism as an outlet for feelings of anger or frustration where they might have become destructive or violent in the past by finding ways to be calm instead, such as meditation.

Others see it more like a religion emphasizing empathy and humanism, where actions should be dictated by how they will affect others rather than what feels right.

The question of how to practice philosophy in the modern day is a central question with complicated answers. There have been many other developments in science during this time, and philosophical questions that were once considered outdated or unimportant have taken on new meanings. A possible way would be to study history of philosophy and its relation to what Western philosophers are dealing with now. There are also more traditional ways like reading essays, discussing theories with people who share your interest, writing, and publishing articles about current topics, etcetera.

Stoic philosophy has been around for centuries, yet it seems to be gaining traction in the modern age. The perspective advocates that one should strive to remain calm and composed in the face of adversity and accept one lot in life without complaint or regret. Stoicism embraces a person's feelings but does not allow them to spiral out of control into depression, leading to suicide or self-harm. Additionally, it encourages people to take responsibility for themselves instead of blaming others when things go wrong, understanding that those who do not learn from mistakes are doomed to repeat them. This philosophy is both empowering and encouraging because it reduces stress by teaching its followers how they can manage difficult situations on their own - rather than demanding help from other people all the time.

Many people think that stoicism is a good philosophy to follow in the modern-day and age. This philosophy contains rules on how one should behave and think about life, death, and anger. It teaches that all misfortunes result in terrible judgment or wrong thinking about things, so if you can control your emotions and avoid superstitions, you will live a happier life free from pain and suffering. However, many people argue against this because they believe it is not helpful in situations like a mental illness. Other approaches may be more beneficial than suppressing feelings through self-discipline or exercise of restraint, such as meditation or yoga.

The ideal stoic for the modern-day and age can be calm, relaxed, and collected while facing adversity. The person should not lose temper when confronted with difficulty in dealing with people or events. They must control their anger and keep a level head even though they may feel like it is impossible. When faced with an obstacle or hardship, this person would have the ability to take action rather than react out-of-character. This type of Stoic will have a firm grasp on logic and know how to use reason to guide every decision.

What should an ideal Stoic practice?

For one, they should be wary of fear and desire because these are what lead people astray in life. One must also strive to live according to nature and not let false beliefs distort that purpose. Finally, a correct stoic practices self-control by embracing all that happens while remaining detached from things outside of their control. This aspect includes accepting death without mourning it or fearing it happening again tomorrow or next year."

Stoicism teaches that people should be indifferent to external events such as wealth, poverty, health, or sickness. One of their principles was "follow nature," which means we should live according to our human nature and not do anything unnatural like following social convention (to follow society) just for its own sake. The stoic view on death is that it is natural and not worth fearing since it will happen sooner or later anyway, so why worry about it?

Stoic Philosophers, on the other hand, have a unique way of looking at death. They believe that people should accept the inevitable and embrace it as welcoming someone into their home. The Stoics feel that there is nothing to be afraid of when you die because everything will go back to the way it was before, with no one able to remember what happened in between. Death for them is mere "the dissolution of the soul from its union with the body."

The stoic response to death is not fear. It is the complete opposite: acceptance. Stoics believe death is a natural part of life and should be greeted as such. This response can seem hard for many people who have never encountered this philosophy before, but after hearing about how their beliefs work, it will make more sense why they do not fear death as most other people do.

Stoics also believe in being indifferent towards events outside of one's control (material possessions, good or bad fortune). This insight elaborates on the thought that you should remain calm no matter what because those things cannot ruin your inner peace unless you want them to. The next time something terrible occurs to someone else, think about what the stoic response would be: "This is unfortunate."

Being at a funeral can make people feel very sad and emotional. Some people may believe that it is wrong to go if they feel indifferent to the person who died. However, Stoics would argue that keeping your feelings in check while still being present acknowledges that you deeply care about the deceased. It doesn't mean you deny any emotion; instead, it means you control yourself and acknowledge your emotions without letting them take over.

Stoics also renounce negative emotions such as pain, fear, or anger because they claim these feelings cloud logical thought. They also recommend achieving happiness because even if one lives a happy life but dies unhappily, he will regret his deathbed for not having lived an emotionally fulfilling life.

Nowadays, as information becomes more accessible than ever before, it can be hard to stay disciplined with some of the distractions the internet providers, such as social media or YouTube videos. Luckily there are tools like exercises and mindfulness meditation available for people to practice Stoicism even in this modern age.

The Stoics had control over their emotions and thought those were much more valuable than material possessions. This type of belief system might have flown back when they first started teaching it - when people did not go around on airplanes every day or live on top of each other like ants, so there were not many external factors causing stress. In the modern-day, though- where we are constantly bombarded by information from social media/TV/radio- it becomes difficult to practice stoicism without being entirely out of touch with reality.

It is hard enough just trying not to get sucked into our screens all day!

Modern Stoicism can apply to anything from dealing with anger management issues to personal problems. It offers a systematic approach for analyzing oneself and one's actions and learning how to make better decisions through those analyses.

Stoic Ethics theory is based on four cardinal virtues: wisdom or prudence, courage or fortitude, justice or self-control, and temperance or moderation; these are also called the "cardinal virtues." The three primary practices of Stoic philosophy study (reading), meditation (contemplation), and writing&mdash: or otherwise known as reflection."

Modern stoicism focuses on mental clarity over emotional control, which was not something that people living in antiquity would have been concerned with; they lived a very different life than we do now. These days, we are much more likely to be overwhelmed with stress than ancient Romans. That is why it makes sense that modern Stoics do not emphasize what their predecessors did when people had more patience for emotions such as anger or anxiety back then.

In ancient times Stoics were very serious about their philosophy, and they just practiced it in solitude. They made themselves scarce with others so that they could live life without distraction. However, this is because Stoicism is not a theory or an idea- it is more like a way of life that you put into practice every day, no matter what happens- good or bad.

Psychology is a large field that studies the human mind and behavior. Psychologists study personality, emotions, attitudes, intelligence, and mental processes to better understand how people think or behave. On the other hand, psychotherapy focuses mainly on getting help with specific anxiety, depression, or addiction. Therapists use different techniques to teach clients the skills they need in order to feel better. One of these techniques is cognitive therapy, which looks at patterns of thought and challenging them when required to be more favorable for you.

The ancient Stoics understood that if you were to live a good life, you have to control how you respond to circumstances. This is because they believe what makes one happy or unhappy are the things outside of their control. The Stoic has no concern with material goods like status and money because they cannot change anything about how they feel. They also have no concern for public praise or criticism since not everyone will agree with what they do. Instead, they focus on achieving inner tranquility that can only come from seeing all events as happening due to fate and letting go of any emotional attachment.

The idea that we control our own emotions and choose how to act on them is a central principle of Stoicism that we have discussed to great lengths in this book. It comes from the Greek stoa meaning "porch or colonnade" or "passageway." The word was first used for a building where people gathered and talked about life, morality, philosophy, politics, and other essential topics.

Stoicism has been adapted to fit contemporary living, such as achieving continual personal growth and peacefulness through observing one's thoughts and actions, rather than quiet resignation to one's fate. Being able to be stoic can help us get through life with fewer regrets because we will have taken responsibility for our happiness instead of relying on others or society at large for it.

Its philosophers taught that feelings are not accurate indicators of what is good or bad. Circumstances do not determine one's happiness; an individual's reactions to external events can be controlled. People need to distinguish between those things they have control over and those they do not; human beings should also try to accept what cannot be helped and what they can control.

Stoicism can be seen as providing a balance between social intelligence (the conscious use of one's intellect to manage relationships) and emotional intelligence (the perception of feelings). For instance, it encourages someone who might be struggling with negativity from another person not to react in anger but instead look for ways to help the other person without sacrificing their happiness or dignity.

This is a philosophy that was popularized in the ancient world for a reason. It has been studied and practiced by leaders such as Marcus Aurelius, Seneca, and Emperors like Nero. It mainly teaches people to control their emotions and resist external events with the tranquility of mind. This philosophy is often considered an alternative to society's emphasis on self-expression.

The Stoics were a school of ancient philosophy that believed the universe was organized by a rational and providential power permeating all of nature. They believed that this power was called Zeus. To them, this god was seen as the driving force behind everything in existence, including human beings. There are many writings from Seneca (a Roman Stoic philosopher) about his beliefs on Zeus and how he saw his presence in everyday life.

"The happiness and serenity we attain through wisdom are not derived from some rarefied air or abstract thought," noted Epictetus. "It comes about as a consequence of what you do with your everyday concerns." What type of mindset goes against this view?

Well, that answer is relatively easy to understand. Ideals against the notion of the cardinal virtues talked about in this book is a clear indication of ideals that work against Stoicism.

Seneca did believe that the universe was organized by a rational and providential power permeating all of nature, which the Stoics identified with Zeus. He felt that humans had a divine spark or fragment of cosmic fire within themselves, which could be nurtured to make them contented with their lives no matter what they might encounter in life – even death itself!

In this day and age, Stoicism has been thrust into the limelight as a way to revitalize personal well-being. However, in essence, Stoicism refers to its ancient philosophy dating back to 300 BC. It teaches people how to live good lives in a universe where they are not guaranteed any control over events. The critical idea of Stoicism is "learning how not suffer fools gladly."

In modern times, many people have taken up the practice of Stoicism with great success by applying some of its core principles like

- Being mindful about your feelings,
- Doing things for yourself rather than someone else all the time, and
- Accepting that whatever happens cannot be changed or influenced by you alone.

Stoics were not allowed to indulge in Ego or Vanity when practicing Stoicism. They had to be mindful that others were doing the same and making sure they did not become too self-centered. They also had to avoid entertaining thoughts about what could have been because it would lead them towards extreme feelings of envy or despair.

After reading this book, a question one might have is: what would Stoicism look like as a philosophy twenty years from now. The answer to that is not an easy one. It might become a popular philosophical movement in universities, with professors lecturing about theories and students taking notes. Alternatively, it may be something completely different--perhaps Stoicism will go out of style entirely; maybe it will be replaced by new philosophies like existentialism or nihilism. The one thing we can say for sure is this: Stoicism will not remain unchanged from today to 20 years from now.

Conclusion

Stoicism is one of the most positive philosophies that exist. It seeks to invite people towards a more desirable way to live gradually, and once done, it releases them from the shackles of emotional turmoil for good. The main concern is achieving external freedom in thought and action by exploring one's emotions as objectively as possible. This book offers clarity in comprehension coupled with control over their execution. By mastering oneself, they instead become impervious to life's threats or immediate excitement, but with just enough consciousness on how both sides have an equally rational nature so long, you do not let your heart dominate your head –

This guide includes three things, the storm before the calm, the oceanic feeling, and what it means to be a stoic. This book is straightforward to read but arduous to finish because of its solid foundation in history and philosophy that gives you firsthand experience using its practices. Like reading a mathematical equation, this workbook will change your perspective on how you perceive life.

We wanted to give the reader the ability to read from any section of the book and still find the information gripping. Because stoicism has many virtues, you will want to read back on, maybe even do some more in-depth research on as well.

There are no original texts from the Stoics. The only way to know what they had to say is by interpreting their work. Some scholars think that Plato's Socratic dialogues influenced them and were likely written before Zeno's time (founder of Stoicism). We can see how Socrates was a prototype for what would become a typical stoic advisor or professor-a guide on life from these dialogues.

What does this mean? We are not sure yet - but it could help us learn more about the origins of philosophy in general!

Philosophy is a field that has shaped the way we think about life and our place in the universe. Today's importance is not necessarily as practical or needed as it was during ancient times, but philosophy still has meaning for us in our modern society. Philosophy helps us understand ourselves better and navigate through the complexities of life with more ease.

Understanding philosophy is a great way to expand your perspective and breadth of knowledge. A lot goes into the study, including logic, skepticism, metaphysics, epistemology, ontology, etc.

There are also many generalizations as to why someone would want to practice philosophy. One might be interested in the process of thinking through a problem or question and the various ways it can be done. Another could find value in increasing their knowledge of how people think about themselves and others by learning more about different philosophical schools and approaches.

Since some people enjoy studying how humans behave around each other, they may also be drawn to philosophy because it considers what one person thinks and what another person thinks. Both perspectives considering what is right or wrong. This study helps us better comprehend why we do things, which may give us perspective into our behavior to improve it for the better if needed.

Philosophy is a word that can be narrowed down to several meanings. It can mean the love of wisdom, an inquiry into truth or fact, and intellectual discourse about unintelligible topics (called "metaphysics").

Many people may not think that studying philosophy in school would be beneficial, but it has many benefits. The first benefit is a more excellent knowledge of oneself. People who study philosophy are taught how to examine their thoughts and beliefs critically. They learn how to question themselves and what they believe in finding the answers they are looking for (and disbelieve). Another benefit is becoming more mindful of your everyday life since you're examining yourself daily as well! To conclude, philosophy is not something you should study just because someone tells you to, but being aware of what is happening around us will always help us make better decisions than if we were not paying attention.

Stoicism is not just an abstract philosophy written by a few men. Since ancient Greece and Rome, its tenets have been practiced when philosophies were more focused on practical application in daily life than today. It is one of the most popular schools of thought because it sees the world through logic rather than emotions, which many people find to be much less taxing for their mental faculties. Stoics believe that we can learn to control our thoughts and feelings to negatively impact us as deeply or frequently as they might otherwise do.

We have talked in great lengths about one thing repeatedly, which is not to be impacted dramatically by our negative emotions. Why was it vital for us to talk about this repetitively? The answer is simple: we are human with a fully functioning brain, so of course, our feelings will impact how we act towards ourselves and others. However, there are steps you can take to help reduce these impacts on your life. One fundamental way is understanding the types of thoughts that lead you down the spiral path of negativity: thinking things like "I am never good enough" or "nothing ever goes my way." These thoughts often make people feel helpless, which only leads them even deeper into a negative mindset where they stop trying their hardest at all aspects of their lives because they believe nothing will work out anyways. It seems more comfortable just to give up than keep fighting against something inevitable happening again.

When practicing Stoicism, we learn significantly about why we should not let emotions cloud our judgments. The first way in which this is true is that it can lead to bad decisions. If a person becomes angry at someone else for something they did and the anger clouds their judgment, they might end up doing something rash that will only make matters worse. Another reason why emotions are problematic when making judgments is that certain feelings cause people to misinterpret what they see or hear. For example, some people become jealous and start seeing other persons as having done untrue things and then react accordingly out of anger- often with disastrous effects on others around them or themselves. This aspect directs us to our finishing point. If you feel any emotion strongly enough, it will cloud your judgment so much that you'll completely lose objectivity over the situation at hand; despite all the previous points we have made.

Learning not to be significantly affected by emotions is essential, strictly because it clouds your objectivity and ability for clear judgment. You are less likely to make errors, which could lead to an unfavorable outcome if you were more objective in the situation.

We trust that this book has accommodated you better understand Stoicism, one of the most influential schools of thought in ancient Greece and Rome.

Thank you!

Before you go, I just wanted to say thank you for purchasing my book.

You could have picked from dozens of other books on the same topic but you took a chance and chose this one.

So, a HUGE thanks to you for getting this book and for reading all the way to the end.

Now I wanted to ask you for a small favor. **Could you please consider posting a review on the platform? Reviews are one of the easiest ways to support the work of independent authors like me.**

This feedback will help me continue to write the type of books that will help you get the results you want.

So if you enjoyed it, please let me know by scanning the QR code below.

Marcus Epictetus

Check Out My Other Books

Below you'll find some of my other popular books on Amazon and Kindle. Check them out by scanning the QR code below.

Made in United States
Orlando, FL
05 September 2024